Paradox

Paradox

◆

The Psychology of Spirituality Workbook

By
Daniel J. Christiano, Ph.D.
with
Robert Curtis, O.P.L.

Writers Club Press
New York Lincoln Shanghai

Paradox
The Psychology of Spirituality Workbook

Writers Club Press
an imprint of iUniverse, Inc.

For information address:
iUniverse, Inc.
2021 Pine Lake Road, Suite 100
Lincoln, NE 68512
www.iuniverse.com

ISBN: 0-595-26411-5

Printed in the United States of America

Contents

Note

This workbook is a companion to the text <u>Paradox: the Psychology of Spirituality</u>. It is designed as an independent daily journal in order to allow the reader to chart the progress of his or her reading and subsequent reflection. The workbook should be utilized only after the chapter and the case studies are read, but before the subsequent chapters are read. During the week after the chapter is read and the journal is being filled in, a suggestion would be to look at the recommended reading list in order to supplement increased knowledge and awareness.

1

Journal

Journal

1. Keep a daily journal for at least one week and address these questions each day:

Day One

a. Did I feel the happiest alone or with someone else today?

_____
_____
_____

b. Did I feel close to anyone today? Was I comfortable?

_____
_____
_____

c. Did I let others know how I felt today? What I needed?

_____
_____
_____

d. How much physical and/or personal space did I need today to feel safe, content, etc:

_____
_____
_____
_____
_____

e. Did I give everyone else enough personal space today? My spouse, my children?

_____
_____
_____
_____
_____

f. Was it difficult for me to set limits with anyone today? Tell what my rules or expectations are? How about accepting any of the limits they set?

_____
_____
_____
_____
_____

g. How aware am I of myself or someone else being emotionally, physically, or sexually abused? What is abuse?

_____
_____
_____
_____

h. Did I feel empty inside today, as if something or someone was missing?

_____
_____
_____
_____
_____

i. Are there any groups that I wish I was part of today? Why?

_____

_____

_____

_____

_____

j. If I were stranded and needed help, who could have been there today for me? Or I for them?

_____

_____

_____

_____

_____

k. Did I feel that being with someone else reduced my time to grow as a person?

_____

_____

_____

_____

_____

Day Two

a. Did I feel the happiest alone or with someone else today?

_____

_____

_____

b. Did I feel close to anyone today? Was I comfortable?

_____

_____

_____

c. Did I let others know today how I felt? What I needed?

_____

_____

_____

d. How much physical and/or personal space did I need today to feel safe, content, etc.?

_____

_____

_____

_____

e. Did I give everyone else enough personal space today? My spouse, my children?

_____

_____

_____

_____

_____

f. Was it difficult for me to set limits with anyone today? Tell what my rules or expectations are? How about accepting any of the limits they set?

_____

_____

_____

_____

_____

g. How aware am I of myself or someone else being emotionally, physically, or sexually abused? What is abuse?

_____

_____

_____

_____

_____

h. Did I feel empty inside today as if something or someone was missing?

_____

_____

_____

_____

_____

i. Are there any groups that I wish I was part of today? Why?

_____

_____

_____

_____

_____

j. If I were stranded and needed help, who could have been there today for me? Or I for them?

_____

_____

_____

_____

_____

k. Did I feel that being with someone else reduced my time to grow as a person?

_____

_____

_____

_____

_____

Day Three

a. Did I feel the happiest alone or with someone else today?

_____

_____

_____

b. Did I feel close to anyone today? Was I comfortable?

_____

_____

_____

c. Did I let others know today how I felt? What I needed?

_____

_____

_____

d. How much physical and/or personal space did I need today to feel safe, content, etc.?

_____

_____

_____

e. Did I give everyone else enough personal space today? My spouse, my children?

_____

_____

_____

_____

_____

f. Was it difficult for me to set limits with anyone today? Tell what my rules or expectations are? How about accepting any of the limits they set?

_____

_____

_____

_____

_____

g. How aware am I of myself or someone else being emotionally, physically, or sexually abused? What is abuse?

_____

_____

_____

_____

_____

h. Did I feel empty inside today as if something or someone was missing?

_____

_____

_____

_____

_____

i. Are there any groups that I wish I was part of today? Why?

_____

_____

_____

_____

j. If I were stranded and needed help, who could have been there today for me? Or I for them?

_____

_____

_____

_____

_____

k. Did I feel that being with someone else reduced my time to grow as a person?

_____

_____

_____

_____

_____

Day Four

a. Did I feel the happiest alone or with someone else today?

_____

_____

_____

b. Did I feel close to anyone today? Was I comfortable?

_____

_____

_____

c. Did I let others know today how I felt? What I needed?

_____

_____

_____

d. How much physical and/or personal space did I need today to feel safe, content, etc.

_____

_____

_____

_____

e. Did I give everyone else enough personal space today? My spouse, my children?

_____

_____

_____

_____

_____

f. Was it difficult for me to set limits with anyone today? Tell what my rules or expectations are? How about accepting any of the limits they set?

_____

_____

_____

_____

_____

g. How aware am I of myself or someone else being emotionally, physically, or sexually abused? What is abuse?

_____

_____

_____

_____

_____

h. Did I feel empty inside today as if something or someone was missing?

_____

_____

_____

_____

_____

i. Are there any groups that I wish I was part of today? Why?

_____

_____

_____

_____

_____

j. If I were stranded and needed help, who could have been there today for me? Or I for them?

_____

_____

_____

_____

_____

k. Did I feel that being with someone else reduced my time to grow as a person?

_____

_____

_____

_____

_____

Day Five

a. Did I feel the happiest alone or with someone else today?

_____

_____

_____

b. Did I feel close to anyone today? Was I comfortable?

_____

_____

_____

c. Did I let others know today how I felt? What I needed?

_____

_____

_____

d. How much physical and/or personal space did I need today to feel safe, content, etc.

_____

_____

_____

_____

_____

e. Did I give everyone else enough personal space today? My spouse, my children?

_____

_____

_____

_____

f. Was it difficult for me to set limits with anyone today? Tell what my rules or expectations are? How about accepting any of the limits they set?

_____

_____

_____

_____

_____

g. How aware am I of myself or someone else being emotionally, physically, or sexually abused? What is abuse?

_____

_____

_____

_____

_____

h. Did I feel empty inside today as if something or someone was missing?

_____

_____

_____

_____

_____

i. Are there any groups that I wish I was part of today? Why?

_____

_____

_____

_____

j. If I were stranded and needed help, who could have been there today for me? Or I for them?

_____

_____

_____

_____

_____

k. Did I feel that being with someone else reduced my time to grow as a person?

_____

_____

_____

_____

_____

Day Six

a. Did I feel the happiest alone or with someone else today?

_____

_____

_____

b. Did I feel close to anyone today? Was I comfortable?

_____

_____

_____

c. Did I let others know today how I felt? What I needed?

_____

_____

_____

d. How much physical and/or personal space did I need today to feel safe, content, etc.

_____

_____

_____

_____

e. Did I give everyone else enough personal space today? My spouse, my children?

_____

_____

_____

_____

f. Was it difficult for me to set limits with anyone today? Tell what my rules or expectations are? How about accepting any of the limits they set?

_____

_____

_____

_____

_____

g. How aware am I of myself or someone else being emotionally, physically, or sexually abused? What is abuse?

_____

_____

_____

_____

_____

h. Did I feel empty inside today as if something or someone was missing?

_____

_____

_____

_____

_____

i. Are there any groups that I wish I was part of today? Why?

_____

_____

_____

_____

_____

j. If I were stranded and needed help, who could have been there today for me? Or I for them?

_____

_____

_____

_____

_____

k. Did I feel that being with someone else reduced my time to grow as a person?

_____

_____

_____

_____

_____

Day Seven

a. Did I feel the happiest alone or with someone else today?

_____

_____

_____

b. Did I feel close to anyone today? Was I comfortable?

_____

_____

_____

c. Did I let others know today how I felt? What I needed?

_____

_____

_____

d. How much physical and/or personal space did I need today to feel safe, content, etc.

_____

_____

_____

_____

_____

e. Did I give everyone else enough personal space today? My spouse, my children?

_____

_____

_____

_____

f. Was it difficult for me to set limits with anyone today? Tell what my rules or expectations are? How about accepting any of the limits they set?

_____

_____

_____

_____

_____

g. How aware am I of myself or someone else being emotionally, physically, or sexually abused? What is abuse?

_____

_____

_____

_____

_____

h. Did I feel empty inside today as if something or someone was missing?

_____

_____

_____

_____

_____

i. Are there any groups that I wish I was part of today? Why?

_____

_____

_____

_____

j. If I were stranded and needed help, who could have been there today for me? Or I for them?

_____

_____

_____

_____

_____

k. Did I feel that being with someone else reduced my time to grow as a person?

_____

_____

_____

_____

_____

Journal—Week End

2. At the end of the week, address the following questions:

a. Ask yourself "who, what, when and where" did I have feelings and beliefs about being alone, with others, setting limits, having personal space in which to grow, etc.?

_____
_____
_____
_____
_____

b. Did certain people help me or hinder me to find myself this week? If so who?

_____
_____
_____
_____
_____

c. Are there certain situations where I didn't feel comfortable? Did I lose myself in those situations? Betray who I am?

_____
_____
_____
_____
_____

3. Develop an action plan to help grow and become the person you want to be. Eliminate any obstacles (persons, places, or things) which keep you from feeling better about yourself or how you spend your time.

_____
_____
_____
_____
_____
_____
_____
_____
_____

4. Think about your relationship to God? Do you believe in His mercy? Do you believe that you are a sacred being?

_____
_____
_____

5. Read the following passages from sacred scripture: (Genesis 1:26–27 and Romans 9:14) Think about what they mean to you and write it down.

_____
_____
_____
_____
_____
_____

6. How do you think you can increase your relationship with God?
Prayer, Mass, works of charity, scripture?

_____

_____

_____

_____

_____

2

Journal

Journal

1. Keep a daily journal for at least one week and address these questions each day:

Day One

a. What are my beliefs about change?

_____
_____
_____
_____
_____

b. Have there been any changes in my life today? Big ones, little ones?

_____
_____
_____
_____
_____

c. Do changes annoy me or excite me?

_____
_____
_____
_____
_____

d. Which changes today brought me what I wanted? How about changes that brought me what I did not want?

_____

_____

_____

_____

_____

e. What changes in my life today were under my control? Someone else's control?

_____

_____

_____

_____

_____

f. What part of my life ended when something new happened today? What part of my life is just beginning because of changes I made?

_____

_____

_____

_____

_____

_____

_____

Day Two

a. What are my beliefs about change?

_____
_____
_____
_____
_____

b. Have there been any changes in my life today? Big ones, little ones?

_____
_____
_____
_____
_____
_____

c. Do changes annoy me or excite me?

_____
_____
_____
_____
_____

d. Which changes today brought me what I wanted? How about changes that brought me what I did not want?

_____
_____
_____
_____
_____

e. What changes in my life today were under my control? Someone else's control?

_____

_____

_____

_____

_____

_____

_____

f. What part of my life ended when something new happened today? What part of my life is just beginning because of changes I made?

_____

_____

_____

_____

_____

_____

Day Three

a. What are my beliefs about change?

_____
_____
_____
_____
_____

b. Have there been any changes in my life today? Big ones, little ones?

_____
_____
_____
_____
_____

c. Do changes annoy me or excite me?

_____
_____
_____
_____
_____

d. Today which changes brought me what I wanted? How about changes that brought me what I did not want?

_____
_____
_____
_____

e. What changes in my life today were under my control? Someone else's control?

_____

_____

_____

_____

_____

_____

_____

f. What part of my life ended when something new happened today? What part of my life is just beginning because of changes I made today?

_____

_____

_____

_____

_____

_____

_____

Day Four

a. What are my beliefs about change?

_____
_____
_____
_____
_____

b. Have there been any changes in my life today? Big ones, little ones?

_____
_____
_____
_____
_____

c. Do changes annoy me or excite me?

_____
_____
_____
_____
_____

d. Today which changes brought me what I wanted? How about changes that brought me what I did not want?

_____
_____
_____
_____
_____
_____

e. What changes in my life today were under my control? Someone else's control?

_____

_____

_____

_____

_____

_____

_____

_____

f. What part of my life ended when something new happened today? What part of my life is just beginning because of changes I made?

_____

_____

_____

_____

_____

_____

_____

Day Five

a. What are my beliefs about change?

_____
_____
_____
_____
_____

b. Have there been any changes in my life today? Big ones, little ones?

_____
_____
_____
_____
_____

c. Do changes annoy me or excite me?

_____
_____
_____
_____
_____

d. Today which changes brought me what I wanted? How about changes that brought me what I did not want?

_____
_____
_____
_____
_____

e. What changes in my life today were under my control? Someone else's control?

_____

_____

_____

_____

_____

f. What part of my life ended when something new happened today? What part of my life is just beginning because of changes I made?

_____

_____

_____

_____

Day Six

a. What are my beliefs about change?

_____
_____
_____
_____
_____

b. Have there been any changes in my life today? Big ones, little ones?

_____
_____
_____
_____
_____
_____
_____

c. Do changes annoy me or excite me?

_____
_____
_____
_____

d. Today which changes brought me what I wanted? How about changes that brought me what I did not want?

_____
_____
_____
_____
_____

e. What changes in my life today were under my control? Someone else's control?

_____

_____

_____

_____

_____

f. What part of my life ended when something new happened today? What part of my life is just beginning because of changes I made?

_____

_____

_____

_____

_____

Day Seven

a. What are my beliefs about change?

_____
_____
_____
_____
_____

b. Have there been any changes in my life today? Big ones, little ones?

_____
_____
_____
_____
_____

c. Do changes annoy me or excite me?

_____
_____
_____
_____
_____

d. Today which changes brought me what I wanted? How about changes that brought me what I did not want?

_____
_____
_____
_____
_____

e. What changes in my life today were under my control? Someone else's control?

_____

_____

_____

_____

_____

f. What part of my life ended when something new happened today? What part of my life is just beginning because of changes I made?

_____

_____

_____

_____

_____

Journal—Week End

2. At the end of the week, ask yourself whether your beliefs about change are the same. Why or why not?

_____

_____

_____

_____

_____

3. At the end of the week ask yourself what makes any change easy to accept or difficult to accept. How did the changes you make in your life effect your growth and the growth of others this week?

_____

_____

_____

_____

_____

_____

_____

4. Develop an action plan to help you make the changes you wish or need. Identify what you need to do. What steps should be taken? What help will you need from others? Get any suggestions you might need from the people you love and trust.

_____

_____

_____

_____

_____

_____

_____

5. How is the development of your own spirituality proceeding? Do you read sacred scripture regularly? Do you pray regularly? Do you participate in the sacraments on a regular basis?

_____

_____

_____

_____

_____

_____

_____

6. Develop an action plan to fold spiritual events into the course of your daily life.

_____

_____

_____

_____

_____

_____

_____

_____

7. Read the following passage from sacred scripture: (Romans 6:3–4) Think about what they mean to you and write it down.

_____

_____

_____

_____

_____

_____

8. What ways do you think you will be able to let go of your old life and engage a new one in Christ?

_____

_____

_____

_____

_____

_____

_____

3

Journal

Journal

1. Keep a daily journal for at least one week and address these questions each day:

Day One

a. How many choices did I make today? Did I have alternatives to choose from? What value or beliefs were reflected by the choices I made?

_____

_____

_____

_____

_____

_____

b. How free did I feel today? What would I do differently today?

_____

_____

_____

_____

_____

c. How much of my past affected the choices I made today?

_____

_____

_____

_____

d. In what ways did I give up my freedom today? For whom, for what, when?

_____

_____

_____

_____

_____

e. Am I as free when I am alone as when I am with someone else?

_____

_____

_____

_____

_____

_____

Day Two

a. How many choices did I make today? Did I have alternatives to choose from? What value or beliefs were reflected by the choices I made?

_____
_____
_____
_____
_____

b. How free did I feel today? What would I do differently today?

_____
_____
_____
_____

c. How much of my past affected the choices I made today?

_____
_____
_____
_____

d. In what ways did I give up my freedom today? For whom, for what, when?

_____
_____
_____
_____

e. Am I as free when I am alone as when I am with someone else?

_____

_____

_____

_____

_____

Day Three

a. How many choices did I make today? Did I have alternatives to choose from? What value or beliefs were reflected by the choices I made?

_____

_____

_____

_____

_____

b. How free did I feel today? What would I do differently today?

_____

_____

_____

_____

_____

c. How much of my past affected the choices I made today?

_____

_____

_____

_____

_____

d. In what ways did I give up my freedom today? For whom, for what, when?

_____

_____

_____

_____

_____

e. Am I as free when I am alone as when I am with someone else?

_____
_____
_____
_____
_____

Day Four

a. How many choices did I make today? Did I have alternatives to choose from? What value or beliefs were reflected by the choices I made?

_____
_____
_____
_____
_____

b. How free did I feel today? What would I do differently today?

_____
_____
_____
_____
_____

c. How much of my past affected the choices I made today?

_____
_____
_____
_____
_____

d. In what ways did I give up my freedom today? For whom, for what, when?

_____
_____
_____
_____
_____

e. Am I as free when I am alone as when I am with someone else?

_____

_____

_____

_____

_____

Day Five

a. How many choices did I make today? Did I have alternatives to choose from? What value or beliefs were reflected by the choices I made?

_____
_____
_____
_____
_____

b. How free did I feel today? What would I do differently today?

_____
_____
_____
_____
_____

c. How much of my past affected the choices I made today?

_____
_____
_____
_____
_____

d. In what ways did I give up my freedom today? For whom, for what, when?

_____
_____
_____
_____
_____

e. Am I as free when I am alone as when I am with someone else?

_____

_____

_____

_____

_____

Day Six

a. How many choices did I make today? Did I have alternatives to choose from? What value or beliefs were reflected by the choices I made?

_____

_____

_____

_____

_____

b. How free did I feel today? What would I do differently today?

_____

_____

_____

_____

_____

c. How much of my past affected the choices I made today?

_____

_____

_____

_____

_____

d. In what ways did I give up my freedom today? For whom, for what, when?

_____

_____

_____

_____

_____

e. Am I as free when I am alone as when I am with someone else?

_____

_____

_____

_____

_____

Day Seven

a. How many choices did I make today? Did I have alternatives to choose from? What value or beliefs were reflected by the choices I made?

_____
_____
_____
_____
_____

b. How free did I feel today? What would I do differently today?

_____
_____
_____
_____
_____

c. How much of my past affected the choices I made today?

_____
_____
_____
_____
_____

d. In what ways did I give up my freedom today? For whom, for what, when?

_____
_____
_____
_____

e. Am I as free when I am alone as when I am with someone else?

_____

_____

_____

_____

_____

Journal—Week End

2. At the end of the week, examine what areas of your life you feel the most free and experience the most choice. Identify those areas of your life that you feel trapped in and unable to change. Are there any choices that you can make now, in the future, when? What areas of your life can you choose to accept rather than change?

_____

_____

_____

_____

_____

_____

_____

_____

_____

_____

_____

_____

_____

_____

3. Develop an action plan to help you experience as much personal freedom as you can. Proceed to change the things that you are able to an can offer you immediate success. After changing those areas of your life, identify other areas which might require different choices on your part. Consider the likelihood of success in each situation and save the most difficult one for last.

_____

_____

_____

_____

4. Read the following passages from Scripture: (2 Corinthians 6:3, 2 Corinthians 3:17) What do you believe these passages mean to you with regards to choices and freedom?

_____
_____
_____
_____
_____
_____

5. How do you place obstacles in front of yourself and others that prevent you from achieving freedom in Christ?

_____
_____
_____
_____
_____
_____
_____

6. How might you overcome obstacles that will allow you to pursue the freedom of Christ?

_____
_____
_____
_____
_____

4

Journal

Journal

1. Keep a daily journal for at least one week and address these questions each day:

Day One

a. How "complete" or "fulfilled" do I feel today? What do I admire about myself? What do I admire about my spouse, significant other, child? Do they make me feel fulfilled?

_____
_____
_____
_____
_____
_____
_____

b. How do I view others who are "just like me?"

_____
_____
_____
_____
_____

c. Do I frequently see a "part" of myself in others that are in my life? Parts I like or dislike about myself?

_____
_____
_____
_____
_____

d. Describe your day and the cast of characters that appeared on stage. Which role did you play? Who was the hero, the villain, side-kick, etc.?

_____

_____

_____

_____

_____

_____

_____

_____

e. Did you "fall in love" today with some part of yourself that you thought was buried or difficult to find? Did you "fall in love" with someone else?

_____

_____

_____

_____

_____

_____

_____

_____

Day Two

a. How "complete" or "fulfilled" do I feel today? What do I admire about myself? What do I admire about my spouse, significant other, child? Do they make me feel fulfilled?

_____

_____

_____

_____

_____

_____

_____

b. How do I view others who are "just like me?"

_____

_____

_____

_____

_____

_____

c. Do I frequently see a "part" of myself in others that are in my life? Parts I like or dislike about myself?

_____

_____

_____

_____

_____

_____

d. Describe your day and the cast of characters that appeared on stage. Which role did you play? Who was the hero, the villain, side-kick, etc.?

_____

_____

_____

_____

_____

_____

_____

_____

_____

e. Did you "fall in love" today with some part of yourself that you thought was buried or difficult to find? Did you "fall in love" with someone else?

_____

_____

_____

_____

_____

_____

_____

_____

_____

Day Three

a. How "complete" or "fulfilled" do I feel today? What do I admire about myself? What do I admire about my spouse, significant other, child? Do they make me feel fulfilled?

_____

_____

_____

_____

_____

_____

_____

b. How do I view others who are "just like me?"

_____

_____

_____

_____

_____

_____

c. Do I frequently see a "part" of myself in others that is in my life? Parts I like or dislike about myself?

_____

_____

_____

_____

_____

_____

d. Describe your day and the cast of characters that appeared on stage. Which role did you play? Who was the hero, the villain, side-kick, etc.?

_____

_____

_____

_____

_____

_____

_____

_____

_____

e. Did you "fall in love" today with some part of yourself that you thought was buried or difficult to find? Did you "fall in love" with someone else?

_____

_____

_____

_____

_____

_____

_____

_____

_____

Day Four

a. How "complete" or "fulfilled" do I feel today? What do I admire about myself? What do I admire about my spouse, significant other, child? Do they make me feel fulfilled?

_____
_____
_____
_____
_____
_____
_____

b. How do I view others who are "just like me?"

_____
_____
_____
_____
_____
_____
_____

c. Do I frequently see a "part" of myself in others that are in my life? Parts I like or dislike about myself?

_____
_____
_____
_____
_____
_____
_____

d. Describe your day and the cast of characters that appeared on stage. Which role did you play? Who was the hero, the villain, side-kick, etc.?

_____

_____

_____

_____

_____

_____

_____

_____

e. Did you "fall in love" today with some part of yourself that you thought was buried or difficult to find? Did you "fall in love" with someone else?

_____

_____

_____

_____

_____

_____

_____

_____

_____

Day Five

a. How "complete" or "fulfilled" do I feel today? What do I admire about myself? What do I admire about my spouse, significant other, child? Do they make me feel fulfilled?

_____

_____

_____

_____

_____

_____

_____

_____

b. How do I view others who are "just like me?"

_____

_____

_____

_____

_____

_____

c. Do I frequently see a "part" of myself in others that are in my life? Parts I like or dislike about myself?

_____

_____

_____

_____

_____

_____

d. Describe your day and the cast of characters that appeared on stage. Which role did you play? Who was the hero, the villain, side-kick, etc.?

_____

_____

_____

_____

_____

_____

_____

_____

_____

e. Did you "fall in love" today with some part of yourself that you thought was buried or difficult to find? Did you "fall in love" with someone else?

_____

_____

_____

_____

_____

_____

_____

_____

_____

Day Six

a. How "complete" or "fulfilled" do I feel today? What do I admire about myself? What do I admire about my spouse, significant other, child? Do they make me feel fulfilled?

_____
_____
_____
_____
_____
_____
_____

b. How do I view others who are "just like me?"

_____
_____
_____
_____
_____
_____

c. Do I frequently see a "part" of myself in others that are in my life? Parts I like or dislike about myself?

_____
_____
_____
_____
_____

d. Describe your day and the cast of characters that appeared on stage. Which role did you play? Who was the hero, the villain, side-kick, etc.?

_____

_____

_____

_____

_____

_____

_____

_____

e. Did you "fall in love" today with some part of yourself that you thought was buried or difficult to find? Did you "fall in love" with someone else?

_____

_____

_____

_____

_____

_____

_____

_____

Day Seven

a. How "complete" or "fulfilled" do I feel today? What do I admire about myself? What do I admire about my spouse, significant other, child? Do they make me feel fulfilled?

_____
_____
_____
_____
_____
_____
_____

b. How do I view others who are "just like me?"

_____
_____
_____
_____
_____
_____
_____

c. Do I frequently see a "part" of myself in others that are in my life? Parts I like or dislike about myself?

_____
_____
_____
_____
_____
_____
_____

d. Describe your day and the cast of characters that appeared on stage. Which role did you play? Who was the hero, the villain, side-kick, etc.?

_____

_____

_____

_____

_____

_____

_____

_____

e. Did you "fall in love" today with some part of yourself that you thought buried or difficult to find? Did you "fall in love" with someone else?

_____

_____

_____

_____

_____

_____

_____

Journal—Week End

2. At the end of the week, ask yourself how much of your casting was real or imagined: Were the characters believable?

_____

_____

_____

_____

_____

_____

_____

_____

3. Things to do for pleasure:

a. Close your eyes and use your imagination and picture in your mind's eye a person who looks like you—but has all the qualities you possess plus all the ones you wish you had. Describe this person to yourself and someone you trust. Describe what they would be doing in life, how they view choices, and how they want to grow. Then imagine becoming that person by embracing them in your arms.

_____

_____

_____

_____

_____

_____

_____

_____

b. Choose several books or movies that you have enjoyed recently and pretend that you and your family and friends were cast into the roles. Which role would you cast yourself in, how about your loved ones?

_____

_____

_____

_____

_____

_____

c. How has the presence of God enriched your life this week?

_____

_____

_____

_____

_____

_____

_____

5

Journal

Journal

1. Keep a daily journal for at least one week and address these questions each day:

Day One

a. How many times did I say or hear the words "love" today? How was the word used? Did I mean it? Did someone else mean it when they said it?

_____
_____
_____
_____
_____
_____
_____

b. Do I have to do anything to be loved by the people I love? Do I expect anything from the people in my life?

_____
_____
_____
_____

c. What "strings are attached" to what I give or receive in my relationships?

_____
_____
_____
_____

d. Did I give freely or did I feel forced to give something today that I did not wish to give?

_____

_____

_____

_____

_____

e. How do I know that I am loved? How do others know that I love them?

_____

_____

_____

_____

_____

f. Who could teach me how to love and be loved?

_____

_____

_____

_____

_____

g. Who first taught me conditional love (or the type of love you must earn)? Was it at home, school, church, etc.

_____

_____

_____

_____

_____

h. Who first taught me unconditional love (or the type of love that is given for just being who you are)?

_____

_____

_____

_____

_____

i. Have I taught anyone today what unconditional love is? How was I able to do this?

_____

_____

_____

_____

_____

Day Two

a. How many times did I say or hear the words "love" today? How was the word used? Did I mean it? Did someone else mean it when they said it?

_____

_____

_____

_____

_____

_____

_____

b. Do I have to do anything to be loved by the people I love? Do I expect anything from the people in my life?

_____

_____

_____

_____

_____

_____

_____

c. What "strings are attached" to what I give or receive in my relationships?

_____

_____

_____

_____

_____

d. Did I give freely or did I feel forced to give something today that I did not wish to give?

_____

_____

_____

_____

_____

e. How do I know that I am loved? How do others know that I love them?

_____

_____

_____

_____

_____

g. Who could teach me how to love and be loved?

_____

_____

_____

_____

_____

h. Who first taught me conditional love (or the type of love you must earn)? Was it at home, school, church, etc.

_____

_____

_____

_____

_____

i. Who first taught me unconditional love (or the type of love that is given for just being who you are)?

_____

_____

_____

_____

_____

j. Have I taught anyone today what unconditional love is? How was I able to do this?

_____

_____

_____

_____

_____

Day Three

a. How many times did I say or hear the words "love" today? How was the word used? Did I mean it? Did someone else mean it when they said it?

_____

_____

_____

_____

_____

_____

_____

b. Do I have to do anything to be loved by the people I love? Do I expect anything from the people in my life?

_____

_____

_____

_____

_____

_____

c. What "strings are attached" to what I give or receive in my relationships?

_____

_____

_____

_____

_____

d. Did I give freely or did I feel forced to give something today that I did not wish to give?

_____
_____
_____
_____
_____

e. How do I know that I am loved? How do others know that I love them?

_____
_____
_____
_____
_____

f. Who could teach me how to love and be loved?

_____
_____
_____
_____
_____

g. Who first taught me conditional love (or the type of love you must earn)? Was it at home, school, church, etc.

_____
_____
_____
_____
_____

h. Who first taught me unconditional love (or the type of love that is given for just being who you are)?

_____

_____

_____

_____

_____

i. Have I taught anyone today what unconditional love is? How was I able to do this?

_____

_____

_____

_____

_____

Day Four

a. How many times did I say or hear the words "love" today? How was the word used? Did I mean it? Did someone else mean it when they said it?

_____

_____

_____

_____

_____

_____

_____

b. Do I have to do anything to be loved by the people I love? Do I expect anything from the people in my life?

_____

_____

_____

_____

_____

_____

_____

c. What "strings are attached" to what I give or receive in my relationships?

_____

_____

_____

_____

_____

d. Did I give freely or did I feel forced to give something today that I did not wish to give?

_____

_____

_____

_____

_____

e. How do I know that I am loved? How do others know that I love them?

_____

_____

_____

_____

_____

f. Who could teach me how to love and be loved?

_____

_____

_____

_____

_____

g. Who first taught me conditional love (or the type of love you must earn)? Was it at home, school, church, etc.

_____

_____

_____

_____

_____

h. Who first taught me unconditional love (or the type of love that is given for just being who you are)?

_____

_____

_____

_____

_____

i. Have I taught anyone today what unconditional love is? How was I able to do this?

_____

_____

_____

_____

_____

Day Five

a. How many times did I say or hear the words "love" today? How was the word used? Did I mean it? Did someone else mean it when they said it?

_____
_____
_____
_____
_____
_____
_____

b. Do I have to do anything to be loved by the people I love? Do I expect anything from the people in my life?

_____
_____
_____
_____
_____
_____
_____

c. What "strings are attached" to what I give or receive in my relationships?

_____
_____
_____
_____
_____

d. Did I give freely or did I feel forced to give something today that I did not wish to give?

_____

_____

_____

_____

_____

e. How do I know that I am loved? How do others know that I love them?

_____

_____

_____

_____

_____

f. Who could teach me how to love and be loved?

_____

_____

_____

_____

_____

g. Who first taught me conditional love (or the type of love you must earn)? Was it at home, school, church, etc.

_____

_____

_____

_____

_____

h. Who first taught me unconditional love (or the type of love that is given for just being who you are)?

_____

_____

_____

_____

_____

i. Have I taught anyone today what unconditional love is? How was I able to do this?

_____

_____

_____

_____

_____

_____

_____

_____

_____

_____

Day Six

a. How many times did I say or hear the words "love" today? How was the word used? Did I mean it? Did someone else mean it when they said it?

_____

_____

_____

_____

_____

_____

_____

b. Do I have to do anything to be loved by the people I love? Do I expect anything from the people in my life?

_____

_____

_____

_____

_____

_____

_____

c. What "strings are attached" to what I give or receive in my relationships?

_____

_____

_____

_____

d. Did I give freely or did I feel forced to give something today that I did not wish to give?

_____
_____
_____
_____
_____

e. How do I know that I am loved? How do others know that I love them?

_____
_____
_____
_____
_____

f. Who could teach me how to love and be loved?

_____
_____
_____
_____
_____

g. Who first taught me conditional love (or the type of love you must earn)? Was it at home, school, church, etc.

_____
_____
_____
_____
_____

h. Who first taught me unconditional love (or the type of love that is given for just being who you are)?

_____

_____

_____

_____

_____

i. Have I taught anyone today what unconditional love is? How was I able to do this?

_____

_____

_____

_____

_____

_____

_____

_____

Day Seven

a. How many times did I say or hear the words "love" today? How was the word used? Did I mean it? Did someone else mean it when they said it?

---

b. Do I have to do anything to be loved by the people I love? Do I expect anything from the people in my life?

---

c. What "strings are attached" to what I give or receive in my relation-ships?

---

d. Did I give freely or did I feel forced to give something today that I did not wish to give?

_____

_____

_____

_____

_____

e. How do I know that I am loved? How do others know that I love them?

_____

_____

_____

_____

_____

f. Who could teach me how to love and be loved?

_____

_____

_____

_____

_____

g. Who first taught me conditional love (or the type of love you must earn)? Was it at home, school, church, etc.

_____

_____

_____

_____

_____

h. Who first taught me unconditional love (or the type of love that is given for just being who you are)?

_____

_____

_____

_____

_____

i. Have I taught anyone today what unconditional love is? How was I able to do this?

_____

_____

_____

_____

_____

_____

_____

_____

_____

_____

_____

_____

Journal—Week End

2. At the end of the week, ask yourself "Who, what, when and where" did I feel loved and give love unconditionally. What obstacles did I create or someone else create to prevent unconditional love? At work, home with my family, with friends, with strangers?

_____
_____
_____
_____
_____
_____
_____
_____
_____
_____

3. Develop an action plan to identify ways to help people grow through love! Identify ways to give people choices at work, school, and home. Identify ways to validate others, whether they agree with you or not. Identify ways to let others know how you feel about them and ways of providing supportive feedback to others without reducing their self-esteem.

_____
_____
_____
_____
_____
_____
_____
_____
_____

4. Think about God's unconditional love in terms of your own shortcomings. How can you emulate God's unconditional love by accepting
someone in your life with their own shortcomings?

_____

_____

_____

_____

_____

_____

_____

_____

_____

_____

_____

_____

0-595-26411-5

www.ingramcontent.com/pod-product-compliance
Lightning Source LLC
Chambersburg PA
CBHW020311290526
45784CB00003B/1461